LIBERTY!
How the Revolutionary War Began

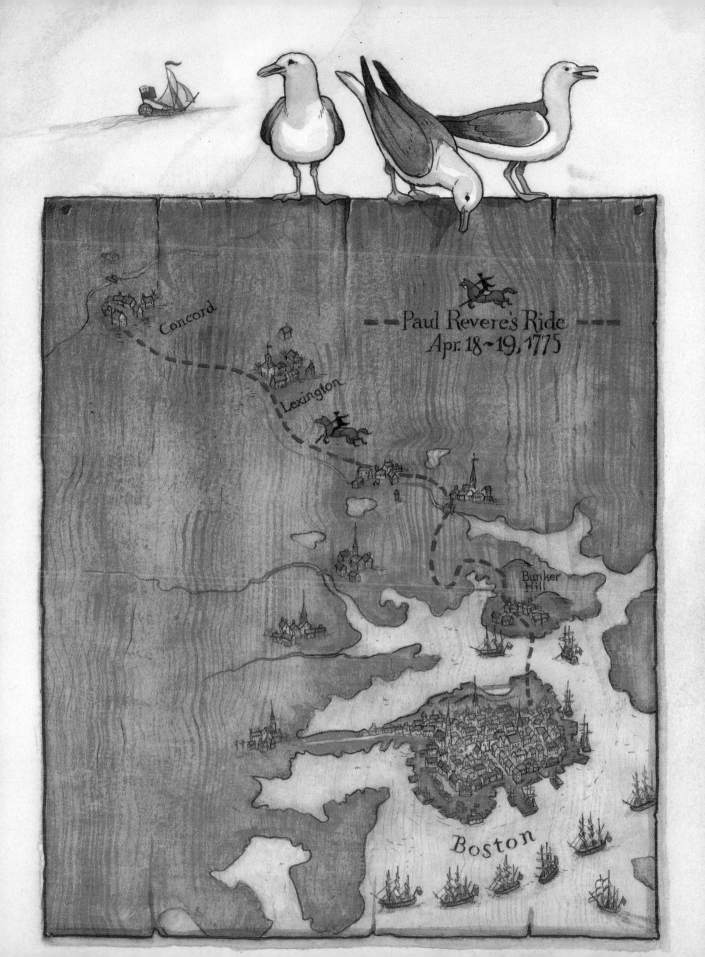

Paul Revere's Ride
Apr. 18~19, 1775

Concord

Lexington

Bunker Hill

Boston

Landmark Books® Grades 2 and Up

LIBERTY!
How the Revolutionary War Began

Lucille Recht Penner ❧ illustrated by David Wenzel

Landmark Books®

Random House 🏠 New York

To Ben

℘*L.R.P.*

Dedicated to everybody who finds wonderment and direction from our diverse past

℘*D.W.*

First Landmark Books® edition, 2002.
Text copyright © 1998 by Lucille Recht Penner.
Illustrations copyright © 1998 by David Wenzel.
All rights reserved under International and Pan-American Copyright Conventions. Published in the United States by Random House, Inc., New York, and simultaneously in Canada by Random House of Canada Limited, Toronto.
Originally published in slightly different form under the title *The Liberty Tree* by Random House, Inc., in 1998. Cover art courtesy of Bettmann/CORBIS.

www.randomhouse.com/kids

Library of Congress Cataloging-in-Publication Data
Penner, Lucille Recht. Liberty! : how the revolutionary war began / by Lucille Recht Penner ; illustrated by David Wenzel.   p.   cm. — (Landmark books)   Includes index.
ISBN 0-375-82200-3
1. United States—History—Revolution, 1775–1783—Causes.   2. United States—History—Revolution, 1775–1783—Campaigns. 3. United States—History—Revolution, 1775–1783—Pictorial works. I. Title. II. Series: Landmark books.   E210.P45   1997   973.3'I—dc20   95-23715

Printed in the United States of America   July 2002   10 9 8 7 6 5 4 3 2
RANDOM HOUSE and colophon and LANDMARK BOOKS and colophon are registered trademarks of Random House, Inc.

Contents

✺ The Liberty Tree ✺

"Long live the king!"

That was the favorite toast of Englishmen in the seventeenth and eighteenth centuries. Even the ones who had left England and sailed across the Atlantic Ocean to live in America.

Why had they left home?

Some left in search of religious freedom. The king and most Englishmen belonged to the Church of England. People who tried to worship differently were thrown in prison or even hanged.

Others left because they were poor and hungry. They hoped to find jobs and food in America.

And some hoped to grow rich. In England, a poor farmer couldn't become a respected landowner. If your parents were poor, you too would probably be poor all your life. But in America, if you worked hard, you might become one of the richest people in the land.

Who were the Americans? Most of them were farmers. Others were shopkeepers and tradesmen. Many were black slaves, who lived mostly in the South.

Some of the "English" colonists were really Dutch, Swedish, or German. But they lived as subjects of the English king.

Colonial men and boys ate with their hats on. They took them off only to drink a toast. Their favorite toast was to the health of the king.

It wasn't easy. But it *was* possible. America was the land of liberty.

By the mid-1700s, a huge elm tree in Boston had become the symbol of the new land. It was called the Liberty Tree. The townspeople gathered under its branches for important meetings.

Other towns and villages along the Atlantic coast named trees in honor of the Liberty Tree of Boston. If they didn't have a big enough tree, they put up a tall pole and called it the Liberty Pole.

The colonists were still proud to be subjects of the king of England, even though he ruled them from 3,000 miles across the ocean. But they were very glad to live in the new and wonderful land of opportunity—America.

In 1760, a new king, George III, came to the throne of England. George liked simple food—boiled mutton and turnips—and enjoyed working in his gardens. Some people called him "Farmer George." Others called him "the royal button-maker" because he loved mechanical inventions.

♋ Help! ♋

"Gee-up!"

On horseback, on foot, and in wagons pulled by oxen, English colonists set out to find new homes.

It was exciting to be a pioneer farmer. But settlers who made their homes on the frontier were always afraid of Indian attacks.

The first English settlers—the Pilgrims—had made peace with the Indians. But some of the settlers who came later treated the Indians rudely and damaged their land. They cut down trees, fenced in fields, and killed or frightened away wild birds and animals.

Finally, the Indians struck back. They joined the French in a war of terror against English settlers. Flaming arrows flew through the dark night. Many lonely farmhouses—and sometimes even whole towns—burned to the ground. Men, women, and children were killed or made the slaves of Indian tribes.

The English settlers needed help!

They had a powerful ally—England. They called England the "Mother Country." The American colonies were England's children. Now that her children were in danger, the Mother Country sent soldiers to help the settlers' own troops defend the colonies against their enemies.

This fight, called the French and Indian War, began in 1754 and continued for almost ten years. At last the French and their Indian allies were defeated. In 1763, a peace treaty—the Treaty of Paris—was signed. France lost almost all her possessions in North America. Britain got Canada and most of the French lands east of the Mississippi.

The colonial soldiers hung up their muskets over their fireplaces and went back to their farms. They hoped they would never have to fight again.

As the war grew fiercer, English colonists began offering bounties for Indian scalps. Bounty hunters sometimes showed off by wearing wigs made of scalps.

By the year 1733, there were thirteen English colonies strung out along the Atlantic coast of North America. Beyond them loomed the thick, dark forest.

George Washington—who later became the first president of the United States—fought in the French and Indian War. "I heard the bullets whistle," he wrote to his brother, "and believe me, there is something charming in the sound."

～ Sneaky Taxes ～

The bloody French and Indian War was finally over.

But what if the Indians attacked again? What if Spain tried to invade?

The British were still afraid of losing their colonies. So they decided to keep an army in America. Ten thousand British soldiers—called "redcoats" because of their red jackets—were sent across the ocean.

Ten thousand men ate a lot of food! And they wore out hundreds of pairs of shoes and suits of clothing. Who would pay for their keep?

The British said the colonists should pay. The British Parliament, which made laws for Britain and its colonies, passed the Quartering Act. It said that the colonists had to provide quarters—places to live—for all the redcoats stationed in America.

Then the British thought of another way to raise money from the colonies. They would enforce the Navigation Acts, which had been passed in the 1600s but never implemented. The Navigation Acts said that the colonists had to buy almost everything they needed from Britain—even when a product could be bought more cheaply from some other country.

Why couldn't the British raise money at home? The British people were already heavily taxed. There was even a tax on windows. So poor people bricked up their windows to avoid paying the tax.

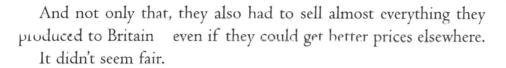

And not only that, they also had to sell almost everything they produced to Britain—even if they could get better prices elsewhere.

It didn't seem fair.

So people paid smugglers to bring in illegal foreign goods and to sell the colonies' own goods to other countries. They did business with their butcher, their baker—and their smuggler!

When the British saw what was going on, they sent warships to patrol the American coast. Smugglers who were caught were fined and imprisoned.

This made the colonists angry.

The Sugar Act made them even angrier. This act made it very expensive for the colonists to import one of their favorite products—molasses.

The Quartering Act, the Navigation Acts, and the Sugar Act seemed to the colonists like sneaky ways of making Britain richer—at their expense!

In addition to providing soldiers with a place to live, the Quartering Act made colonists responsible for furnishing each redcoat with candles, fuel, salt, bedding, and beer.

One day, a British customs officer seized a ship carrying an illegal cargo of molasses. He left some of his men in charge of the ship and went for help. When he returned, the cargo was gone. So were the ship's sails, anchors, and ropes! Forty armed men with blackened faces, he was told, had carried them off.

❧ The Death-Head Stamp ❧

The Stamp Act of 1765 was the last straw!

Parliament had passed a new tax. Now every piece of paper that changed hands in the colonies—every newspaper, marriage license, will, diploma, and land deed—had to carry a British stamp before it could be considered legal. And the colonists had to pay for these stamps.

People were furious! Riots broke out in Boston. In other cities there were demonstrations and violent speeches against the British. To many, the Stamp Act seemed like the death of liberty.

Americans didn't mind paying taxes to their *local* governments. That seemed fair because they elected their own representatives. But there was nobody to represent them in the British Parliament.

If a stamp tax collector refused to resign, he was sometimes chased out of town by a mob carrying clubs and throwing stones.

The colonists drew stamps with a skull and crossbones. This was to show their belief that the Stamp Act was the death of liberty.

Who were the Sons of Liberty?

They were groups of men opposed to Britain's treatment of the colonies. Some were poor, uneducated workers. Others were wealthy merchants, lawyers, and teachers. Not all of them believed in mob violence, but the threat of it scared their opponents.

The Stamp Act was taxation without representation! It could not be allowed.

Groups of angry men formed bands called the Sons of Liberty. They burst into the homes of stamp tax collectors and warned them to resign. If a stamp tax collector refused, the Sons of Liberty threw rocks through his precious windows—glass was very expensive. If he still held out, they smashed his house and all his belongings.

Naturally, hardly any stamps were sold. Parliament finally gave in and repealed the Stamp Act.

What wonderful news! Bells rang out in every city. People danced in the streets. They cheered and drank toasts to good King George. "Long live the king!" They were sure that the king was on their side. Now they thought America would be treated fairly, at last.

Ebenezer McIntosh, a shoemaker, led a gang that joined the Sons of Liberty. They tore down the houses of stamp tax collectors and other British officials. They were always ready for a fight. McIntosh ran among his men shouting orders through his speaking trumpet.

One night, an effigy of Andrew Oliver—who had been appointed stamp tax collector for Massachusetts—was hung from the Liberty Tree. An effigy of a boot with the devil crawling out of it was also hung from the tree. The boot stood for Lord Bute—a British politician whom the colonists hated. They considered him responsible for the Stamp Act.

John Hancock
(1737–1793) was said
to be the richest man
in Boston. He was also
a loyal Son of Liberty.
Even before the
Revolutionary War
broke out, the British
put him on their
Most Wanted list.

One young man spoke
sneeringly of the
colonies at a quilting
party. The girls grabbed
him, stripped off his
shirt, poured molasses
over his head, and
"feathered" him with the
tips of cattail plants!

❦ Tar and Feathers ❧

"Then join hand in hand, brave Americans all.
By uniting we stand, by dividing we fall."

The colonists had rejoiced too soon.

In 1767, Parliament passed the Townshend Acts. These placed high taxes on tea, cloth, and other British goods.

Americans were furious. "We won't pay," angry men shouted. "We won't buy *anything* from Britain!"

Colonial women refused to wear British cloth or serve tea. Instead, they made rough homespun cloth and drank coffee smuggled in from the Dutch West Indies. Patriotic women swore never to marry a man who bought British goods. And the Sons of Liberty vowed a horrible revenge against anyone who defied the boycott: tar and feathers!

They stripped the offender, poured hot tar over him, and then—to make him look ridiculous—emptied a feather pillow over his head. Feathers stuck to the black tar. The screaming man was carried out of town on a wooden rail and dumped in a ditch.

Soon almost no one would buy British goods.

The British and Americans were already furious at each other when an American ship—the *Liberty*—was seized by British customs agents on a charge of smuggling. The *Liberty* was owned by John Hancock, a rich Boston merchant who supported the Sons of Liberty.

The news spread quickly. Men raced to the docks, a fight broke out, and the customs agents were beaten up.

The British government was outraged at the news. Parliament voted to send troops to get the Americans back under control.

In 1768, a squadron of British warships sailed into Boston Harbor. Seven hundred redcoats marched ashore and pitched their tents on Boston Common.

Being tarred and feathered was a horrible torture. It was feared so much that the Sons of Liberty had only to send a cold ball of tar and feathers to someone in order to terrify him. He would change his behavior or leave town at once.

The finest cloth and needles were made in England. When American women decided to boycott English goods, they held spinning bees. The cloth they made was coarse and unattractive, but they wore it proudly. Since black cloth could be purchased only from Britain, almost everyone stopped wearing black clothes, even to funerals. Instead, a black armband was worn over a person's regular clothes.

❧ Lobsterbacks ❧

"On Friday, September 30, 1768," Paul Revere wrote, "the ships of war arrived. [The soldiers] landed on Long Wharf; they formed and marched with insolent parade, drums beating, fifes playing, up King Street." The sun shone on their brightly polished boots and shining muskets. The redcoats were an impressive sight.

But it wasn't at all comfortable to be a British soldier. Their red wool jackets were hot and itchy. Their white pants were so tight that they had to be put on wet. Then, as they dried, they got even tighter and pinched cruelly.

A redcoat had to pass inspection each morning. Washing wasn't necessary, but he had to shave. He had to clean and polish his boots, buttons, and buckles. Then he braided his hair in a long pigtail,

The uniform wasn't the only discomfort a redcoat endured. He had to carry all his belongings into battle with him. Besides his musket, musket balls, and bayonet, he carried a knapsack stuffed with food, blankets, and camping gear. It was a heavy load.

Sometimes a married redcoat was allowed to bring his wife and children along. They were given a small amount of food. In return, the women cooked, washed, and nursed sick and wounded men. Whenever the redcoats moved to a new camp, their families went with them. Little children were often present when bloody battles took place.

12

powdered it with white flour, and dipped the end in animal grease. He smelled awful!

Soldiering was a terrible life. Redcoats were paid only about eight pence (equal to two cents) a day. If they didn't keep their uniforms clean, they were whipped.

A soldier who tried to desert was likely to be executed. Sometimes he had to stand next to his coffin while the firing squad took aim at him. And if he escaped, Indians might be sent after him with orders to bring back his scalp.

Life in the British army was difficult, and redcoats were certainly not welcomed in Boston. Girls turned up their noses. Men sneered. And little boys ran after groups of red-jacketed soldiers, screaming, "Lobsterbacks! Bloodybacks! Go home!"

A cat-o'-nine-tails was a whip made of nine knotted ropes or leather thongs fastened to a handle. Soldiers were punished by being whipped on their bare backs.

Redcoats received very low pay. To earn extra money, some hired themselves out to farmers and storekeepers in their free hours.

Crispus Attucks was a tall, strong dockhand. He was part black and part Indian. He and his friends called the redcoats names and threatened them with clubs. Attucks was shot in the chest and killed by Hugh Montgomery, a British private.

Two of the redcoats who had fired on the crowd, Matthew Kilroy and Hugh Montgomery, were found guilty of manslaughter. They were branded on the thumb and dismissed from the British army.

❧ The Boston Massacre ❧

"Lobsters! Lobsters for sale!"

Every time a redcoat walked through the streets of Boston he heard angry jeers. Sometimes he felt a quick push from behind and—*splat*—he found himself facedown in a pile of garbage. The redcoats began to hate Boston and everyone in it.

The townspeople hated them right back. British soldiers infuriated the people of Boston by gambling, drinking, and holding noisy parades on the Sabbath.

Finally, on March 5, 1770, the situation exploded.

It was a dark night, cold and snowy. A soldier was standing guard in the sentry box in front of the Customs House. A boy came along and began shouting insults at him. The soldier dashed out of his box and hit the boy with his musket. The boy ran away crying.

But soon he came back with his friends. They threw snowballs at the guard and screamed, "Lousy rascal! Bloodyback!"

A crowd began to gather. The meeting-house bell tolled. Men ran

The redcoats and their officers were bombarded with snowballs stuffed with ice or bits of broken oyster shells.

Each year after the Boston Massacre, the people of Boston marked its anniversary with prayers for the dead and angry speeches against the British. A large meeting was planned for the fifth anniversary. The British officers decided that they would not tolerate strong speeches against their country. They made a plan. A young British officer was to bring an egg to the meeting. If the speeches were unacceptable, he would throw the egg at a woman in the audience. That would be the signal for other British officers to arrest the colonists' leaders. Unfortunately for the British, the young officer fell on his way to the meeting and broke the egg.

No one was arrested.

through the streets calling, "Town-born, turn out!" This cry was usually raised to call townspeople to help fight a fire. In fact, some people thought there *was* a fire. They rushed out of their houses carrying buckets of water. Others were ready to fight. They grabbed fence railings and rocks and ran toward the Customs House.

The terrified sentry shouted for help. Captain Thomas Preston hurried to his side with seven redcoats. They loaded their muskets, lowered their bayonets, and faced the angry crowd.

"Go home," Captain Preston yelled. "The sentry was only doing his duty."

But the crowd screamed insults at the soldiers and pressed closer. Someone smashed a club across Preston's arm. Rocks flew.

Suddenly, a shot rang out. Then another. A man in the crowd dropped down dead. Preston ran among his men, striking up their guns and yelling at them to stop firing. But when the smoke cleared and the crowd withdrew, three men lay dead and two more were dying.

Boston would long remember this terrible night.

Admiral Jon Montague, the commander of the British warships anchored in the harbor, was spending the night in a house on the wharf. When the "Indians" began marching back to town, he opened his window and called, "Well, boys. You have had a fine, pleasant evening. But mind, you'll have to pay the fiddler yet."

An "Indian" yelled back, "Come down, squire, and we'll settle up in two minutes." The admiral slammed his window shut.

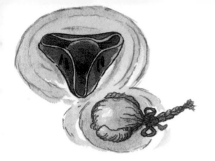

～ Rally, Mohawks! ～

As each "Indian" left the tea ships, a guard searched him to make sure he hadn't stolen any tea. One man had stuffed his pockets with tea leaves. The tea—and the man's hat and wig—was thrown into Boston Harbor.

The children of Boston, whose fathers came home very late with painted faces and feathers in their hats, always remembered the night of the Boston Tea Party. It was a wonderful story to tell their own children and grandchildren.

The morning after the Boston Tea Party, men went out in small boats and beat the piles of tea down with paddles to make it unusable.

The whisper went around on December 16, 1773: "Boston Harbor a teapot tonight."

Everyone who heard the whisper looked out over the water. Three British ships, laden with 90,000 pounds of tea, were riding peacefully at anchor.

After the Boston Massacre, Parliament had repealed the Townshend Acts—except for the tax on tea. Tea was the only British product that the Americans still refused to buy.

Their boycott had helped drive the British East India Company—which imported the tea—to the verge of bankruptcy. So the British prime minister, Lord North, had granted the British East India Company a monopoly on the American tea trade. If Americans had no other choice, he thought, they would give up and buy British tea.

Americans were outraged! If Britain could grant a monopoly on tea, she could grant monopolies on *everything* the colonies needed.

After a fiery protest meeting, a group of colonists dressed up as Indians. They disguised their faces with coal dust and paint, stuck feathers in their hats, and marched two by two down to the waterfront.

At the wharf, they divided into three groups and boarded the tea ships. The sailors handed over the keys to the holds without a fight, and the "Indians" got to work. They hoisted the heavy chests of tea on deck, split each one open, and dumped the loose tea overboard. Then they slipped away.

When the sun rose the next morning, piles of tea could be seen floating on the tide.

This incident became known as the Boston Tea Party. A song about it was sung throughout the colonies:

"Rally, Mohawks! Bring out your axes,
And tell King George we'll pay no taxes
On his foreign tea."

❧ Blows Must Decide! ❧

"Blows must decide!" King George shouted.

He was furious when he heard about the Boston Tea Party. In his royal opinion, Britain should respond with powerful blows of brute force.

Parliament passed new laws designed to govern the colonies more strictly than ever. These laws were so harsh that the colonists bitterly called them the "Intolerable Acts."

And to punish Boston further, British warships arrived on June 1, 1774, to close Boston Harbor.

Church bells tolled from morning to night, public buildings were draped in black, and people mourned. Many Bostonians were sailors, fishermen, merchants, and traders. They made their living from the sea. Boats brought food and supplies into the city.

Would Boston starve?

No! Towns, cities, and colonies all over America rallied to her aid. Soon horse-drawn carts with barrels full of corn, wheat, rice, and fish came streaming into the city. So did cattle, sheep, and goats.

Many colonists were ready to fight, too. A cartload of food from Connecticut came with a letter. "We are ready," it said, "to sprinkle the American altars with our hearts' blood."

And George Washington wrote, "I will raise 1,000 men, subsist them at my own Expense, and march myself at their Head for the relief of Boston!"

Many fights broke out between the redcoats and the people of Boston. When some soldiers tripped a butcher who was carrying a side of beef, his fellow butchers came to the rescue. Soon swords and cudgels were out. One of the poor butchers lost his nose to a sword slash.

A committee was set up to distribute the food sent by friendly colonies. Its members decided that men should be required to work in order to receive a share. One of the jobs they had to do was paving public streets.

The colonists claimed that the redcoats were poor shots. A farmer watched soldiers taking turns firing at a target. None could hit it.

"I could hit it ten times in a row," said the farmer.

The soldiers laughed and gave him a gun. He hit the target every time. In fact, he told the astonished men, his little son could toss up an apple and shoot out all the seeds as it was coming down!

In Farmington, Connecticut, almost 1,000 people attended a meeting to protest the Intolerable Acts. First, they raised a Liberty Pole that was forty-five feet tall. Then the town's public executioner read aloud a copy of the Intolerable Acts. After this, he burned the document to show that Americans would never accept such tyranny.

Four thousand redcoats, under the command of Lieutenant General Thomas Gage, arrived to occupy the city. At first, General Gage thought his job would be easy. But soon he was writing home, "If you think ten thousand men enough, send twenty; if a million is thought enough, give two."

General Gage's first problem was housing his men. Barracks had to be built, but colonial workmen refused to build them. And nobody would sell straw or timber to the hated redcoats.

In fact, the redcoats themselves didn't seem to like their job. Many of them sneaked away and disappeared into the countryside. The Americans welcomed them. British deserters often ended up teaching colonial soldiers how to drill and use arms.

Now the colonists were training daily. War might break out at any moment, and they wanted to be ready.

King George had said it. Blows would decide!

ஃ Country Bumpkins? ஃ

Who had the strongest army in the world?

The British.

If war broke out with the colonies, the British seemed certain to win.

America didn't even have an army. Instead, each colony had a militia—a ragtag assortment of men from sixteen to sixty-five years old—that drilled once a week on village greens. Militiamen were mainly concerned with defending their own villages and colonies. They had no uniforms and little knowledge of war. Some of them didn't even have guns. The British laughed. How could these country bumpkins put up a fight?

Most British officers were gentlemen who had bought their positions. Some wealthy men even bought them for their sons. If his father paid enough money, even a baby could be listed as the commander of a regiment!

In America, the system was different. American militiamen elected their own officers from among their friends and neighbors. They called them by their first names and didn't bother to salute. No one expected it.

Some towns organized alarm companies. These were made up of old men and young boys who would defend the town if it was attacked while the militia was away.

The Brown Bess, a musket used by both the Americans and the British, could be fired rapidly—three or four shots a minute. But it was so hard to aim that no one really tried. A soldier would point it in the general direction of the opposing army, turn his head away in case the gun blew up, and squeeze the trigger. If he was lucky, some of the enemy fell.

Benjamin Franklin suggested that the colonial army use bows and arrows instead of muskets. They were quieter, he said, didn't make clouds of smoke, and required no ammunition.

But nobody took his idea seriously. Later, Franklin organized a smuggling ring in London to supply guns to the colonies.

A gang led by Paul Revere stole guns and cannons from the British. They sneaked them out of Boston and hid them in the countryside.

The Americans could not begin to match the British in equipment. Militiamen had to provide their own weapons. Most had only a musket, a horn to hold gunpowder, a mold for making bullets, and a small supply of ammunition. Officers sometimes carried swords as well.

As war loomed closer, the militias practiced loading their muskets every day. But they didn't practice firing, because they didn't have enough ammunition.

When General Gage's redcoats arrived to punish Boston for the Tea Party, some of the militiamen became minutemen. Minutemen had to keep their weapons ready at all times. They were supposed to be ready to fight with only one minute's warning. The British grew to dread the sight of them. Minutemen seemed to appear from nowhere whenever their drummers sounded the alarm.

Still, if America was really going to fight, what she had to have was a real army. The need came sooner than anyone expected.

✍ Unite or Die ✍

By now, war seemed almost certain. You could practically smell the gunpowder in the air.

The colonies knew very well that Britain could crush them one by one. But if they joined together, maybe they would have a chance. It was unite or die.

The call went out. Delegates from all the colonies were invited to Philadelphia for the First Continental Congress.

Delegates from Massachusetts—including John Adams, who would later become the second president of the United States—set off in a large coach drawn by four horses. As they passed through New Haven, Connecticut, Adams wrote, "All the bells in town were set to ringing, and the people—men, women, and children—were crowding at the doors and windows."

On September 5, 1774, fifty-six delegates met in Philadelphia. Only Georgia didn't send delegates. Georgia, the colony farthest from Massachusetts, was not yet ready to throw off British rule.

Had the moment come to fight for independence? Many of the delegates were sure it had. But others still hoped for peace with Britain.

The First Continental Congress was held in Carpenter's Hall in Philadelphia. It was owned by the city's carpenters, who were proud to be the hosts of this historic meeting.

Liberty or death?

Patrick Henry was a delegate from Virginia and a friend of George Washington. He believed that Americans should fight for their independence. "Is life so dear, or peace so sweet, as to be purchased at the price of chains and slavery?" he asked in a famous speech. "I know not what course others may take; but as for me, give me liberty or give me death!"

During the First Continental Congress, John Adams was often invited to elegant meals at the homes of important Philadelphians. He describes one feast: "Turttle, and every other Thing—Flummery, Jellies, Sweetmeats of 20 sorts, Trifles, Whip'd Syllabubs, floating Islands, fools, etc., and then a Desert of Fruits, Raisins, Almonds, Pears, Peaches—wines most excellent and admirable."

Nonetheless, all of them were angry at the way Massachusetts had been treated. The Continental Congress voted to condemn the Intolerable Acts and passed a bill of rights, listing the freedoms that all Americans had a right to enjoy.

And the Congress agreed on a new boycott of British goods. This boycott was called the Association. No British goods would be purchased or even *used*. And no more slaves would be imported into the United States.

How could the boycott be enforced? Committees of Inspection would be set up in each colony. People caught violating the boycott would be visited by the Sons of Liberty and their pots of hot tar.

Delegates who hoped for peace drew up a petition to King George, asking him to protect the rights of his American subjects. Maybe war with the Mother Country could still be avoided.

But Patrick Henry spoke out boldly in favor of independence. "The distinctions," he cried, "between Virginians, Pennsylvanians, New Yorkers, and New Englanders are no more. *I am not a Virginian, but an American!*"

✎ Spies! ✎

What is a spy?

Someone who secretly watches and gathers information about an enemy's actions and plans.

A spy could be anyone. The young boy who held a British officer's horse might listen to his conversation and report it to the Sons of Liberty.

Some spies memorized the information they gathered so there would be no proof if they got caught. Others hid notes in their shoes, in hollow buttons, and even in bullets.

"Sympathetic ink"—a kind of invisible ink—was used by both sides. So were ciphers and book codes.

Ciphers were easy to write. You just substituted a different letter for each letter of the alphabet. For example, if you sent your friend a message saying T RGLPGB, he would be able to read it—as long as he knew the cipher you were using:

Benedict Arnold was a general in the American army. But he wasn't satisfied. He wanted more pay and a higher rank. He offered to betray his country. He would weaken West Point—a fort under his command—so that the British would be able to capture it. When Americans learned of his treachery, they were shocked. A "Benedict Arnold" became another term for a traitor.

> T stands for A
> R stands for S
> G stands for E
> L stands for C
> P stands for R
> G stands for E (again)
> B stands for T

T RGLPGB would mean A SECRET.

The Darragh family lived in Philadelphia. Lydia Darragh collected information about the British troops, and her husband scribbled it in shorthand on tiny bits of paper. Lydia stuffed the notes into large, hollow buttons and sewed them onto a coat. Her fourteen-year-old son, John, put on the coat, slipped out of Philadelphia, and made his way to George Washington's camp. There he cut off the buttons and gave them to his older brother, Lieutenant Charles Darragh, who handed the information to General Washington.

Nathan Hale was a loyal American. He disguised himself as a schoolmaster, slipped through British lines, and collected a great deal of information. But before he could return, he was arrested and sentenced to be hanged without even a trial. Before the hangman knotted the noose around his neck, Nathan Hale said, "I only regret that I have but one life to lose for my country."

Ann Bates was a Philadelphia schoolteacher who became a British spy. She disguised herself as a peddler, carrying a stock of needles, thread, combs, knives, and medicine.

It wasn't unusual to use a cipher in colonial times. Many people—including Thomas Jefferson—wrote their private letters in cipher. Benjamin Franklin didn't. He said he could never remember the key!

A book code was different from a cipher. The spy and the person to whom he was writing had copies of the same book (usually a dictionary). Numbers were used, and each group of numbers stood for a word. They told where in the book that word could be found. The first number told the page; the second, the line; and the third, which word on the line. The spy would compose the coded message by using his copy of the book. And the other person would figure it out by using *his* copy.

The adventures of many successful spies will always remain secrets. But some famous spies of the Revolutionary War, like Nathan Hale, are still honored for their courage and loyalty. Others, like Benedict Arnold, who betrayed his country, are remembered with scorn.

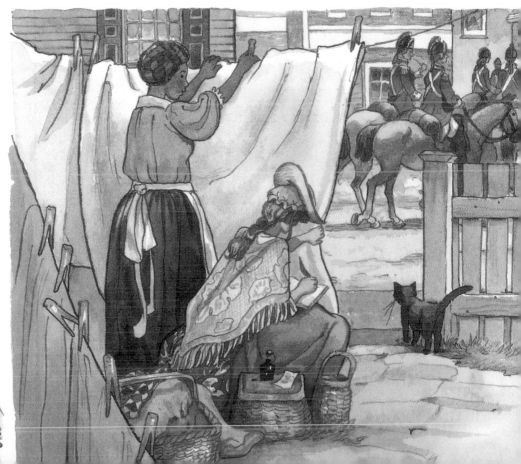

To cross the Charles River, Paul Revere had to pass very close to the *Somerset*, a British man-of-war armed with sixty-four cannons. The least noise might give him away. At the last minute, he thought of wrapping the oars in cloth to muffle their sound. There was no time to waste, so he asked a lady for her petticoat. She threw it down to him from a window. In later years, Paul Revere would tell his grandchildren that when the petticoat fluttered into his hands, it was still warm.

✺ One if by Land, ✺ Two if by Sea

One day, two young men in old brown suits, with red handkerchiefs tied around their necks, strolled out of Boston. They kicked at stones, whistled, and tried to look innocent. But almost everyone they met recognized them for what they were: British spies.

General Gage had ordered spies to scout the countryside toward Lexington and Concord. He thought the colonists had guns and ammunition hidden in the area. And he also suspected that two important leaders of the Sons of Liberty—Samuel Adams and John Hancock—were hiding nearby. It would be a great blow to the colonists' cause if he could capture them. "Until they are sent home prisoners," General Gage wrote, "I fear we shall have no peace."

Finally, his plans were ready. Hoping to surprise the Americans, he gave the order to attack at night on April 18, 1775. But the Americans were ready for him. Two lanterns were hung in the steeple of Old North Church to warn that the redcoats were on the march.

Paul Revere saw the signal, hurried to the Charles River, and was rowed across by a friend. When they reached the other side, Revere borrowed a horse, leaped into the saddle, and galloped off toward Concord to give the alarm.

"The regulars are out!" he yelled, and raced on. The regulars were the British troops. When men heard his shout, they dressed quickly and loaded their muskets.

Meanwhile, the redcoats were hurrying down to the docks. Boats ferried them across the Charles.

At the other side, there wasn't any dock. To reach land, the redcoats had to jump out of their boats into icy water and thick mud. The first men to wade ashore just stood there, freezing and miserable, until all the rest had arrived. Finally, soaked and muddy, the redcoats marched off, shivering, down the dark road to Lexington.

But as they marched, they heard an unwelcome sound. Church bells were tolling. Drums were beating the alarm.

General Gage's secret attack was a secret no more.

The townspeople of Concord buried their guns and ammunition in haystacks and freshly plowed fields so British spies wouldn't see them. When they received warning of a British attack, they would dig them up, arm themselves, and be ready to fight.

∽ The Shot Heard ∽ 'Round the World

The redcoats marched all night, a distance of sixteen miles. When they reached Lexington at dawn on April 19, 1775, they found a ragged line of minutemen drawn up on the village green.

"Ye villains, ye rebels, disperse! Lay down your arms!" shouted Major John Pitcairn, a British officer.

Suddenly, a shot rang out. Nobody knows which side fired it. This was the first shot of the Revolutionary War.

It is known as "The Shot Heard 'Round the World."

Now all the redcoats raised their muskets and blazed away. When the smoke cleared, eight minutemen were dead, and ten wounded. The rest ran for cover.

The redcoats gave three cheers. Then they wheeled around and marched off to Concord. In the center of town, they chopped down the Liberty Pole and burned it. Smoke billowed into the air.

Meanwhile, minutemen had been gathering on a hill beyond a stream. When they saw the rising smoke, they thought the British were setting fire to the town.

Jonathan Harrington was one of the Americans killed on the green at Lexington. He managed to crawl to the doorway of his house—where his wife and son were watching in horror—before dying at their feet.

Many British officers were wounded during the march back to Lexington. Their uniforms made them easy for the minutemen to pick out. The commander of the British troops, Colonel Francis Smith, a very fat man, was wounded in the leg. But he didn't dare get on a horse because he would be an easy target in the saddle. He had to limp along with his men.

They raced toward a bridge that crossed the stream. The redcoats fired a volley across the water, and two Americans were killed.

"Fire, fellow soldiers, for God's sake, fire!" shouted the Americans' commander, Major John Buttrick.

A volley rang out from the Americans. Seconds later, three redcoats were dead and one was dying. At least ten more were wounded. The rest quickly retreated.

The redcoats formed columns and began marching back to Lexington. But the minutemen took a shortcut. They were waiting in ambush on both sides of the narrow road.

Muskets blazed from behind stone walls, barns, bushes, and houses. As the redcoats marched on, the minutemen ran ahead, took up new positions, and fired again. The terrified redcoats began to run. They dashed into Lexington and flung themselves on the ground, gasping for breath.

They were lucky. A British officer, Lord Percy, had just arrived with 1,000 fresh troops. These new arrivals held off the minutemen while the exhausted soldiers rested. Then they began the long march back to Boston.

It was a nightmare. All along the route, minutemen shot at them from ambush. It was dark by the time they finally staggered into town and reached their barracks.

ᕤ Don't Fire Until You See ᕤ the Whites of Their Eyes!

When the sun rose over Boston Harbor on June 17, 1775, sailors on the British warship *Lively* awoke and stretched. Suddenly, one of them shouted in surprise. On a hill across the Charles River from Boston loomed a fort. It had not been there yesterday!

Whistles blew and gunners raced to their battle stations. Soon the *Lively*'s cannons were spitting fire and black smoke. Other British warships joined in.

American militiamen had worked secretly all night to build the fort. Now they crouched behind its walls as the British cannons thundered. The noise was terrifying.

Swarms of redcoats arrived from Boston, crossing the river by boat. They lined up in battle formation on the beach. At any moment they would charge.

The Americans defending the fort were desperately short of ammunition. Some who had just arrived from New Hampshire had had to stop and make bullets out of old pipes on their way into Boston.

Some militiamen were frightened. They avoided danger whenever they could. Once, fifteen men used the excuse of having to help a wounded man to the rear.

Dr. Joseph Warren, a beloved American patriot, died at the Battle of Bunker Hill. His body couldn't be recovered until the British left Boston almost a year later. But Paul Revere was able to identify his skeleton, because he had wired two false teeth into the doctor's mouth not long before he died.

Every shot would have to count. Colonel William Prescott, the American commander, told his men, "Don't fire until you see the whites of their eyes!"

The redcoats trotted up the hill toward the fort, bayonets at the ready. It was absolutely quiet. Suddenly, a stream of gunfire poured out of the fort. The redcoats turned and ran back down the hill.

But when they reached the beach, their officers beat them with swords, forcing them to storm the fort again. And again, a deadly blast of gunfire mowed down the front ranks. The terrified survivors panicked and ran.

The men who were left charged up the hill yet again—and suddenly the firing stopped. The Americans had run out of ammunition. Redcoats swarmed over the walls of the fort, pointing their deadly bayonets. Colonel William Prescott ordered a retreat. He himself was the last to leave the fort.

When the Americans were gone, the British counted their dead. Almost half the soldiers who had set out that morning had been killed or wounded.

The Battle of Bunker Hill showed both sides how terrible war would be. But it was too late to turn back. Even deadlier battles lay ahead.

The British major John Pitcairn—who had fought at Lexington and Concord—was killed during the last charge. He died in the arms of his son, a lieutenant. Altogether, close to a thousand British soldiers died or were wounded in the battle.

✑ Women at War ✑

American women didn't usually fight in the Revolutionary War. But they strongly supported the cause of liberty.

A lady from Philadelphia expressed the feelings of many of her countrywomen when she wrote:

> "My only brother I have sent to the camp with my prayers and blessings…had I twenty sons and brothers they should go. Tea I have not drank since last Christmas, nor bought a new cap or gown…and this way do I throw my mite to the public good. I know this, that as free I can die but once, but as a slave I shall not be worthy of life. I have the pleasure to assure you that these are the sentiments of all my sister Americans."

DEBORAH SAMPSON
A young soldier was wounded in battle. When the doctor examined the wound, he discovered that the soldier was a woman. Her name was Deborah Sampson. Deborah begged the doctor not to give her secret away—and he agreed. She explained that she had wanted very much to fight for American independence. But women were not accepted in the army. So Deborah had disguised herself as a man.

SYBIL LUDINGTON
On the night of April 26, 1777, a messenger on horseback pounded up to the Ludington farm in New York State. He was carrying an important message for Colonel Henry Ludington. British soldiers were planning to attack Danbury, Connecticut, the next day.

Colonel Ludington was not at home. But his sixteen-year-old daughter, Sybil, volunteered to alert her father's troops. She saddled a horse and rode through the countryside all night, knocking on doors and calling out the militiamen.

The next day the British attacked Danbury. They burned the city, but many of their soldiers were killed. The men Sybil had awakened had reached Danbury in time to give the British a real fight.

MOLLY PITCHER

Some women went to war with their husbands. They didn't fight in the battles, but they worked in camp—cooking, cleaning, and nursing the wounded. One such woman was Mary Ludwig, usually called Molly. Her husband was a gunner in the First Pennsylvania Artillery.

On a very hot day in June 1778, an important battle took place—the Battle of Monmouth. The soldiers got very thirsty. Molly took some pitchers to a nearby stream. She filled them with cool water and carried them to the exhausted soldiers while the battle raged around them. The men admired her courage and gave her the nickname "Molly Pitcher."

Later the same day, when Molly's husband collapsed from heatstroke, Molly took his gun and fought for the rest of the battle.

All the soldiers were grateful to Molly. When the war was over, the Pennsylvania Legislature gave her a pension for life.

John Hancock was president of the Second Continental Congress and the first delegate to sign the Declaration of Independence. He wrote his name firmly in large letters. He said, "King George will be able to read *this* without his spectacles!"

His signature became so famous that "John Hancock" has become another term for signature.

✺ The Declaration ✺ of Independence

Thomas Jefferson wrote the Declaration of Independence in two weeks. He worked standing at his writing desk, which was set on a high table.

Independence.

To most Americans, it was a beautiful word, but a frightening one. They wanted freedom. But how could they cut their ties of friendship with, and loyalty to, Britain—the Mother Country?

When the Second Continental Congress gathered in Philadelphia on May 10, 1775, many delegates still hoped to avoid war. They drafted the Olive Branch Petition—an appeal to King George from "his Majesty's faithful subjects in the Colonies." It was a final attempt to solve the problems between America and Britain peacefully.

But the king refused even to receive the Olive Branch Petition. Instead, he announced that the colonies were in a state of rebellion, and readied his forces for war.

Congress also began preparing for war. Because the colonial militias weren't strong enough to meet the British army, Congress authorized the creation of a regular army. And it appointed George Washington "General and Commander-in-Chief of the forces raised and to be raised in defense of American Liberty."

Then the question of independence was discussed. Samuel Adams asked, "Is not America already independent? Why not, then, declare it?" Most delegates agreed with him.

After a long debate, Congress appointed a committee to write a Declaration of Independence. The Declaration was actually written by Thomas Jefferson, who later became the third president of the United States.

Americans had high hopes for the Second Continental Congress. As the delegates from Connecticut rode through New York on their way to the meeting, crowds of people came out to meet them. They unfastened the horses and pulled the carriage through the streets themselves, laughing and cheering.

The unanimous Declaration
∽ Liberty! ∾

In words that are as thrilling today as when they were written in 1776, Jefferson proclaimed the great principles of human freedom:

- All men are created equal.
- They have natural rights, which cannot be taken away from them, to life, liberty, and the pursuit of happiness.
- Government must protect these rights.
- If it doesn't, the people can abolish it and create a new government that will "effect their Safety and Happiness."

Copies of the Declaration of Independence were sent by messenger throughout the colonies. It was read aloud on village greens and from the steps of churches.

In one small town in South Carolina, the only person who knew how to read was a nine-year-old boy. He stood up in front of everyone and read the entire Declaration in a loud, clear voice. His name was Andrew Jackson. Many years later, when he was grown up—and America was independent—he would become the seventh president of the United States.

King George, the Declaration stated, had forced unfair laws and taxes on the colonies. Therefore, they now declared themselves independent!

The Declaration of Independence was approved by the Continental Congress on July 2, 1776, and officially adopted on July 4. When people heard the news, they laughed, cried, cheered, set off firecrackers, rang bells, and danced in the streets.

John Adams wrote to his wife: "I am well aware of the toil, and blood, and treasure, that it will cost us to maintain this declaration, and support and defend these States. Yet, through all the gloom, I can see rays of ravishing light and glory. I can see that…posterity will triumph in that day's transaction."

INDEX

Adams, John, 22, 23, 36
Adams, Samuel, 26, 35
alarm companies, 20
Arnold, Benedict, 24, 25
Association, the, 23
Attucks, Crispus, 14

Bates, Ann, 25
Battle of Bunker Hill, 30–31
Battle of Monmouth, 33
book code, 25
Boston, 3, 8, 11, 13, 14, 15,
    18, 21, 26, 29, 30
Boston Common, 11
Boston Harbor, 17, 18, 30
Boston Massacre, 14–15
Boston Tea Party, 17, 18, 21
British East India Company, 17
Brown Bess, 20
Bute, Lord, 9
Buttrick, Maj. John, 29

Canada, 4
Carpenter's Hall, 22
cat-o'-nine-tails, 13
Charles River, 26, 27, 30
ciphers, 24–25
Committees of Inspection, 23
Concord, Mass., 26, 27
Customs House, 14, 15

Danbury, Conn., 32
Darragh, Charles, 24
Darragh, John, 24
Darragh, Lydia, 24
Declaration of Independence, 34,
    35, 36

Farmington, Conn., 19
First Continental Congress,
    22–23
France, 4
Franklin, Benjamin, 21, 25
French and Indian War, 4–5, 6

Gage, Lt. Gen. Thomas, 19, 21,
    26, 27
George III, 3, 9, 17, 18, 19, 23, 34,
    35, 36

Hale, Nathan, 25
Hancock, John, 10, 11, 26, 34
Harrington, Jonathan, 28
Henry, Patrick, 23

Indians, 4, 13
Intolerable Acts, 18, 19, 23

Jackson, Andrew, 36
Jefferson, Thomas, 25, 35, 36

Kilroy, Matthew, 14

Lexington, Mass., 26, 27, 28, 29
Liberty, the, 11
Liberty Pole, 3, 19, 28
Liberty Tree, 3, 9
Lively, the, 30
Ludington, Col. Henry, 32
Ludington, Sybil, 32
Ludwig, Mary, *see* Molly
    Pitcher

McIntosh, Ebenezer, 9
militias, 20–21, 35
minutemen, 21, 28, 29
Montague, Adm. Jon, 16
Montgomery, Hugh, 14
"Mother Country," 4, 23, 35

Navigation Acts, 6–7
New Haven, Conn., 22
North, Lord, 17

Old North Church, 26
Olive Branch Petition, 35
Oliver, Andrew, 9

Parliament, 6, 8, 9, 11, 17, 18

Percy, Lord, 29
Philadelphia, 22, 23, 35
Pilgrims, 4
Pitcairn, Maj. John, 28, 31
Pitcher, Molly, 33
Prescott, Col. William, 31
Preston, Capt. Thomas, 15

Quartering Act, 6, 7

redcoats, 6, 7, 11, 12–13, 14, 15,
    18, 19, 21, 27, 28, 29, 31
Revere, Paul, 12, 21, 26, 27, 30

Sampson, Deborah, 32
Second Continental Congress,
    34, 35
Shot Heard 'Round the World,
    the, 28
Smith, Col. Francis, 29
smugglers, 7
Somerset, the, 26
Sons of Liberty, 8, 9, 10, 11, 23,
    24, 26
Spain, 6
Stamp Act, 8–9
Sugar Act, 7

tar and feathers, 11
taxes, 6–7, 8–9, 11
toasts, 2
Townshend Acts, 11, 17
Treaty of Paris, 4

Warren, Dr. Joseph, 30
Washington, George, 5, 18, 23,
    24, 35
West Point, 24

Boston

New Haven

New York

Philadelphia

To England —

Atlantic Ocean

N

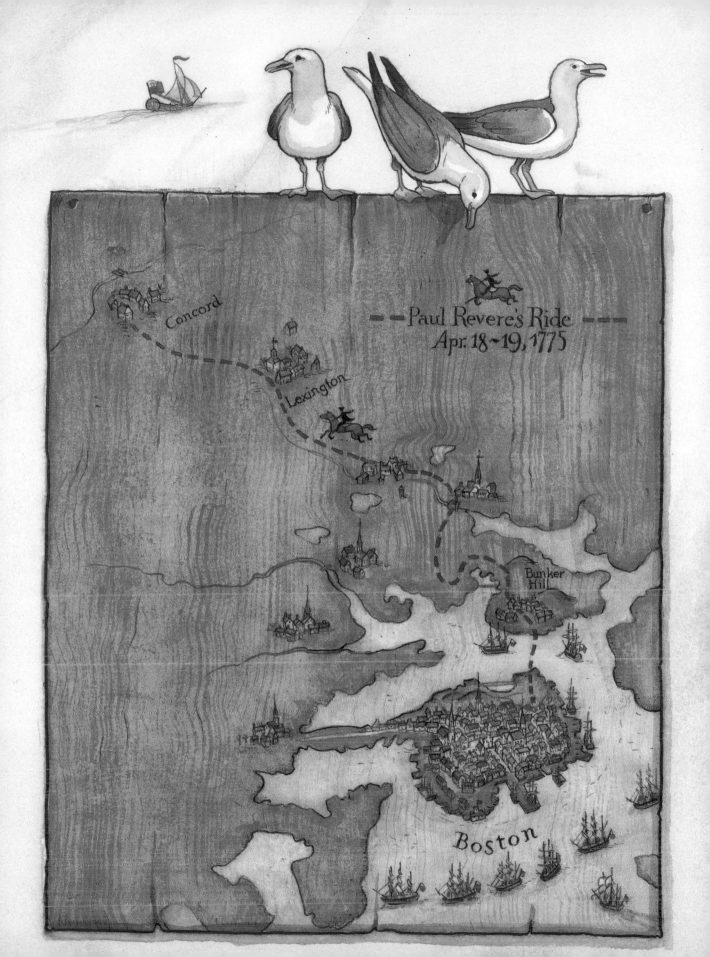

Relive history with Landmark Books®!

Grades 2 and Up

Meet Abraham Lincoln

Meet Benjamin Franklin

Meet Christopher Columbus

Meet George Washington

Meet Thomas Jefferson

Illustrated

Liberty! How the Revolutionary War Began

The Pilgrims at Plymouth

Westward Ho! The Story of the Pioneers

Grades 4 and Up

Meet Martin Luther King, Jr.

Grades 6 and Up

Ain't Gonna Study War No More: The Story of America's Peace Seekers

The Day the Sky Fell: A History of Terrorism

The Landing of the Pilgrims

There Comes a Time: The Struggle for Civil Rights

The Witchcraft of Salem Village